1,000,000 Books

are available to read at

---◆---

www.ForgottenBooks.com

---◆---

Read online
Download PDF
Purchase in print

ISBN 978-0-266-08603-1
PIBN 10947241

1 MONTH OF
FREE
READING

at
www.ForgottenBooks.com

By purchasing this book you are eligible for one month membership to ForgottenBooks.com, giving you unlimited access to our entire collection of over 1,000,000 titles via our web site and mobile apps.

To claim your free month visit:
www.forgottenbooks.com/free947241

English
Français
Deutsche
Italiano
Español
Português

www.forgottenbooks.com

Mythology Photography **Fiction**
Fishing Christianity **Art** Cooking
Essays Buddhism Freemasonry
Medicine **Biology** Music **Ancient**
Egypt Evolution Carpentry Physics
Dance Geology **Mathematics** Fitness
Shakespeare **Folklore** Yoga Marketing
Confidence Immortality Biographies
Poetry **Psychology** Witchcraft
Electronics Chemistry History **Law**
Accounting **Philosophy** Anthropology
Alchemy Drama Quantum Mechanics
Atheism Sexual Health **Ancient History**
Entrepreneurship Languages Sport
Paleontology Needlework Islam
Metaphysics Investment Archaeology
Parenting Statistics Criminology
Motivational

UNITED STATES DEPARTMENT OF AGRICULTURE

MISCELLANEOUS CIRCULAR NO. 38

WASHINGTON, D. C.   FEBRUARY, 1925

THE AGRICULTURAL OUTLOOK FOR 1925

Prepared by the Staff of the Bureau of Agricultural Economics

CONTENTS

THE PURPOSE OF THIS REPORT

President Calvin Coolidge in his address at the International Livestock Exposition last December said:

> "Inasmuch as orderly production is a necessary preliminary to orderly marketing, the well-informed farmer must keep himself posted, months in advance, concerning the probable production of various kinds of livestock during the coming season, as well as concerning the probable requirements of the market."

SUMMARY

The general outlook for American agriculture is fairly encouraging this year as compared with recent years, although there may be a slackening in domestic demand for farm products next winter.

Some aspects of the situation should receive special consideration. For the United States as a whole, little change from the production program of 1924 is recommended. Present high prices for wheat are mainly due to low yields in some countries. The indicated winter wheat acreage is somewhat larger than last year, and it is probable that the total world acreage will be at least as large as last year. If the yield in 1925 is normal present prices can not be expected for the 1925 crop.

Growers of spring wheat, especially those who may expect to benefit from the tariff, should be cautious about increasing their acreage over last year. The production of flax, on the other hand, is still somewhat under domestic consumption and flax prices for the 1925 crop will probably be relatively higher than wheat. Some slight shift from wheat to flax, therefore, may be profitable.

A marked shortage of hogs during the coming year appears probable and hog prices should advance to much higher levels. Increased breeding for fall farrowing, therefore, should be profitable. The feeding demand for 1925 feed crops evidently will be smaller than during the present crop year. Corn and oat acreages, therefore, should not be increased especially by farmers who sell their crop.

Continued expansion in the dairy industry has depressed prices of dairy products, and with a growing foreign competition a further increase in the number of dairy cows would probably retard recovery of prices.

A cotton crop as large as last year should be absorbed at sustained prices. Present prices, therefore, should not discourage growers from planting the usual cotton acreage.

Producers of the major farm products should follow a program of balanced and economical production about the same as last year. In general, the higher prices realized for 1924 products were due to reduced production, here or abroad, rather than to any marked improvement in demand. Farmers should continue to devote available resources to the reduction of existing indebtedness rather than to general expansion of production which might result in another period of low returns to farming.

In making plans for 1925, farmers in each section should consider the outlook for all the commodities that they produce or can produce. Though in general, marked shifts in production do not seem advisable, yet each farmer may possibly add to his net income for the year by modifying the acreage of his crop or the numbers of his livestock in the light of the outlook for each of the products he can grow.

A brief summary of the detailed outlook statements, which constitute the main body of this report, follows.

General business prosperity during the first half of this year will maintain the domestic demand for the 1924 farm products yet to be marketed and should stimulate the demand for the better grades of certain farm products. It is not assured, however, that the industrial improvement of the first half of 1925 will continue into 1926 at the same high level.

The foreign market for most American farm products promises to be at least as good as during the past year.

From present indications ample credit for farming purposes will be available in most regions of the United States on more favorable terms. Interest rates are now somewhat lower than in recent years and needed credit should be arranged for early in the season.

The present tendency in industry points to stronger competition for farm labor during the spring and summer of 1925 than prevailed during 1924. From present indications little change in farm equipment and upkeep costs are to be expected.

If there is an average world crop of *wheat* in 1925, the present high price of wheat can not be expected to prevail for the 1925 crop, although prices are likely to be better than in 1923. Growers of hard spring wheat are cautioned not to increase production above domestic requirements.

The shortage in the European crop of *rye* which was a contributing factor in the export demand for wheat does not seem likely to be repeated.

Flax acreage may still be increased somewhat before production with average yields will equal the present consumptive demand, and it seems probable that flax prices in the United States will be on a relatively higher level than wheat during the next crop year if production is below the domestic requirements.

The outlook for *cotton*, although perhaps less favorable than in 1924 from the standpoint of production costs, is otherwise encouraging. From present indications stocks at the end of the current season will not be large and the improved foreign demand should be maintained. Another 13,000,000-bale crop could probably be absorbed at sustained prices.

Hog producers enter 1925 with every indication that prices during the next 18 months will be higher than at any time since 1920. Conditions therefore are favorable for expanding fall farrowings.

While the 1924 *corn* crop will probably be well cleaned up an increased acreage in 1925 does not appear advisable in view of the indicated reduction in the feeding demand.

Immediate prospects for the *cattle industry* appear moderately favorable. Prices for 1925 should average somewhat higher than for 1924, with the decreased supply of pork products as the chief strengthening factor. All conditions indicate that the industry is gradually working into a more favorable position.

Further expansion in *dairying* in 1925 seems inadvisable. An improvement in the prices of dairy products can hardly be expected if the number of cows is increased.

Prospects for the *sheep industry* in 1925 appear favorable. There does not appear to be any immediate danger of overproduction, as the increase in the number of sheep has as yet been only slight.

Although there are as many *horses and mules* of working age on farms as will be needed for the coming season, a decided decline in colt production in past years indicates a shortage in work horses a few years hence. It is believed that on farms where conditions are favorable to colt raising there might well be a somewhat larger number of mares bred in 1925 than in 1924.

The outlook of the *poultry industry* during 1925, from the standpoint of market egg prices is favorable, but from the standpoint of immediate poultry prices it is not so encouraging. Higher prices for other meats and possibly reduced feed costs should increase poultry profits during the latter part of 1925 and early 1926.

Oats production in 1924 was slightly in excess of domestic requirements and with no increase probable in domestic consumption during the next crop year any increase in the oats acreage in 1925 does not seem advisable.

While *barley* prices are at relatively high levels the general situation suggests that last year's acreage was sufficient under normal conditions to produce sufficient barley for domestic requirements and for the limited export demand for malting barley.

The production of *market hay* should be more closely adjusted to the decreasing demand. Production of alfalfa and other legumes might be increased profitably where the local supply is not equal to the consumption.

The supplies of *feedstuffs, forage,* and *manufactured feeds* are apparently sufficient until the new crops become available, and the price trend is more likely to work downward than upward.

The present low price of *potatoes*, which is due to the unusually heavy yield of last year, is likely to result in too small an acreage of potatoes this year. Since exceptionally heavy yield per acre again in 1925 is not probable, a potato acreage about the same as last year should be maintained.

Present high prices for *sweet potatoes* should not influence growers to plant a largely increased acreage of this crop this year.

Any substantial increase in *peanut* acreage in 1925 over that of last year may result in lower prices.

A *bean crop* in 1925 in excess of domestic needs would tend to put the price of the entire crop on an export basis, thus losing to the grower the benefit of the tariff of $1.05 a bushel. If the usual acreage is planted in California in 1925 and other States equal the 1924 acreage, a crop in excess of domestic needs may result.

During 1925 there probably will be a sustained or slightly increased demand for such *vegetables* as *lettuce, celery, spinach,* and *cucumbers*, but little prospect for any increase in the demand for *cabbage* and *onions* and for such staple *canning crops* as *corn* and *tomatoes*. During recent years, however, the production of vegetables has been increasing rather more rapidly than the demand, and the tendency seems to be toward generally lower prices with increasing competition between the various commercial producing sections.

Present conditions indicate that increased plantings of *citrus fruits* and *western grapes* should be discouraged, and that any plantings of *apples, peaches,* and *pears* and other tree fruits should be confined to the best commercial sections and to the gradual replacement of old farm orchards in localities where a good local market seems assured.

Any increase in *tobacco* acreage this year is undesirable, excepting perhaps in some of the flue-cured types. The price outlook for most types of tobacco is better now than last year, but stocks on hand are still large.

Higher prices for *sugar* and *sugar beets* during the coming season are unlikely, because of the probability of a large carry-over of sugar from last year's crop.

Any considerable increase in production of *rice* in the United States is inadvisable. The efforts of rice growers in this country may well be directed toward increasing the quality rather than the quantity of their product.

DOMESTIC DEMAND

General business prosperity during the first half of this year will maintain the domestic demand for the 1924 farm products yet to be marketed and should stimulate the demand for the better grades of certain foods; but the domestic demand for the 1925 crops, from present indications, will be no better than the present demand, if as good.

The year 1925 opened with many factors pointing toward continued progress in business activity for the first half of the year. Agriculture, itself, out of the 1924 crops, is contributing an increased money income of about $500,000,000, which is 4 per cent above the total farm income from the 1923 crop. The improvement is particularly marked in the Wheat and Corn Belts, where about 90 per cent of this increase is found. While contributing to an increased prosperity of the agricultural population in certain sections, too much importance should not be placed upon this moderate improvement. A large proportion of the additional income has already gone to reduce accumulated indebtedness of the past few years.

In addition to improvement in general business due to agriculture, there has been a marked increase in industrial wage earnings as a result of the increase in employment in basic industries, particularly in woolen fabrics, pig iron, and steel production. Building activity remains at a high level. Present easy credit induces further business expansion. The general price trend has been upward since June, 1924, and is now at the level it reached during the period of active business in the spring of 1923. The unusual activity of the stock exchanges since last November indicates further general business prosperity, at least during the first half of this year. Therefore sustained urban demand may be expected for the portion of the 1924 farm products yet to be marketed. Active business with full employment of wage earners at good wages. such as is indicated by the present outlook, will stimulate particularly the demand for certain products like cotton, wool, the better grades of fruits and vegetables, eggs, dairy, and meat products.

Although the factors influencing the demand for the current crop are favorable they do not necessarily indicate the conditions under which the 1925-26 crops will be marketed. It is not assured that the industrial improvement of the first half of 1925 will continue into 1926 at the same high level. Should an overstimulation of business and overproduction of manufactured goods occur in the next few months, there may be expected to follow a reduction in business activity, and, therefore, slackened demand for some of the 1925 farm products.

It is further probable that in the season for marketing the 1925 crop there will be a lessened farmers' total income in certain regions, which, through reducing the demand for industrial products, may reciprocally weaken the urban market for agricultural products. In the Wheat Belt, for example, farmers should not expect a repetition of the unusual situation of 1924: A very good crop in this country and a short crop for the rest of the world. In the Corn Belt, the short crop of hogs will probably be only partially offset by higher prices, while reduced feeding demands for corn will tend to reduce the total value of the corn crop. It is therefore probable that in the Wheat and Corn Belts, which comprise a substantial portion of American agriculture, there will be a diminished income as compared with 1924.

Furthermore, the poorer returns for these sections will not be materially offset by the better conditions in the range and dairy sections, and by the continuation of present conditions in the South. Relatively high prices for many farm products may prevail through 1925, but possible reduction in marketings as compared with 1924 makes it unlikely that income from the 1925 crops will be sufficiently large to continue to support any marked expansion in general industrial activity.

FOREIGN DEMAND

The foreign market for most of the products of the American farmer promises to be at least as good as it has been the past year. For specific products the strength of demand will depend both upon the purchasing power of the most important foreign markets and the competition to be expected in these markets from the most important foreign producers.

The European economic situation is distinctly brighter than it was a year ago. In the great industrial centers of western Europe more confidence is apparent and production has been resumed on a larger scale. Loans from the United States have been largely instrumental in strengthening the financial situation. Employment of labor at increased real wages has increased the purchasing power of agricultural deficit countries. This increased purchasing power, however, does not necessarily mean greater imports of absolute necessities. In the wheat trade, for example, improved economic conditions facilitate trade but may not increase imports or consumption of wheat. Higher purchasing power, however, will improve and develop European markets for products which are not absolute necessities, but which give greater variety to the supply of food and clothing.

Economic improvement is most marked in Germany, where the stabilization of the currency in December, 1923, followed by the acceptance of the Dawes plan appears to have improved credit and revived industry. Employment and real wages have increased nearly to the 1913 level. If this favorable situation continues, Germany should be a good market for American farm products during the next few months. The revival of industry means greater consumption of cotton, of which the United States is the chief source. Short grain crops in 1924 coupled with higher purchasing power in industrial centers and better facilities for financing imports are favorable for continued sales of American wheat and rye, at least, until the next harvest. In spite of increased prices, the demand for American pork products in Germany has continued strong.

The United Kingdom is still suffering from depression in several of its key industries. Textile mills show greater activity but are not yet on a full-time basis. About 1,000,000 workmen in all industries are still listed as unemployed. The British situation, however, is bad rather in relation to pre-war conditions than in comparison with the present situation in continental Europe. Through all the postwar period British credit has been maintained and British people have always been able to purchase almost their normal supplies of farm products possibly excepting cotton and wool. The rise of sterling exchange nearly to par will tend to facilitate purchases during the coming year. The United Kingdom is the most dependable market for American farm products, and in spite of all efforts to favor the Dominions, it is likely to take American pork products, cotton, tobacco, and many other agricultural commodities in approximately the same quantities as in the past. Takings of wheat and flour, however, will depend somewhat upon the size of the Canadian crop.

France and Italy show continued economic improvement. Industries in both countries are generally active; bank deposits show large increases and employment conditions are healthy. France is more self-sufficient agriculturally than either the United Kingdom or Germany and furnishes a dependable market only for cotton and some minor products. Italy buys cotton and also is second only to the United Kingdom in imports of wheat.

In general the present tendency in Europe is toward increased purchasing power in the great industrial centers together with increased production of agricultural products. To a large extent the heavy purchases of agricultural products in the United States by European countries since the war have been due to decreased domestic production of these products. But each year since the war has marked some progress in returning to pre-war production in the countries of central and western Europe. This increase in production which is encouraged by the governments of these countries tends to make them more self-sufficient and to diminish the need for our farm products. Grain production, however, has not recovered in Russia and the Danube Basin and lacking these former sources of supply western Europe must still purchase much greater quantities of grain from overseas than she did before the war. The share of the United States in this greater market will depend upon the strength of competition from such countries as Canada, Argentina, and Australia. As eastern Europe recovers, competition will become still more keen. Producers of wheat especially should watch Russian and Danube conditions closely.

Of non-European markets, the Orient is taking much less wheat and flour this year than last, and is not likely to repeat last year's large imports of American flour unless there is a failure in the 1925 crop in Manchuria and North China. Japan is importing more cotton but less wheat and rice than last year. With its large sugar crop to exchange for our agricultural products, Cuba should be a good market this year, and Mexico shows economic improvement which should increase her purchasing power.

There is no reason to expect any less competition from Argentina, Australia, and Canada than in the past year. High prices for the present wheat crop in Argentina and Australia will certainly stimulate the seeding for the crop of next season in those countries. In Canada the competition will depend upon yields which may be expected to be higher than in 1924. Competition in meat and dairy products promises to be as keen if not keener than last year.

AGRICULTURAL CREDIT

From present indications ample credit for farming purposes will be available in most regions on more favorable terms. Interest rates are now somewhat lower than in recent years, and credit needed should be arranged for early in the season.

Additional credit for production purposes should not be used unless there is fair prospect of increasing thereby the net farm income, or unless essential to bring about sound diversification. Refunding of farm mortgage and short-term loans for longer terms and at lower rates of interest will prove in some instances advantageous. Full advantage should be taken of the improved credit conditions that now prevail and the available Federal credit agencies.

Farmers in general are now in somewhat better position than in recent years to finance their needs. This improvement in the situation is shown in a reduced demand for credit and in the growth of country bank deposits during 1924. The general case in credit conditions is reflected in the low interest rates prevailing during most of the year. Discount rates at Federal reserve banks have continued to decline since 1920 and were at low levels in December, 1924. The interest rate on Federal farm loans is now 5½ per cent, while the Federal intermediate credit bank rate is 4½ per cent for direct loans to cooperative marketing associations and 5 per cent for discounts. Interest rates charged by commercial lending agencies have also declined since 1921.

While credit conditions in general are more favorable, there are some weak spots in the situation. Owing to numerous bank failures present credit agencies in some sections of the country are now inadequate. The breakdown of the old packer-controlled livestock loan companies and the weakened condition of many local banks have aggravated the credit situation in the range country. The funds of the Federal intermediate credit banks are available for sound loans when presented by solvent, well-managed credit agencies. This source of credit should be utilized in so far as possible to supplement the agencies now serving these regions. In the Cotton Belt efforts to reduce the amount of merchant credit for production purposes continue with resulting lower costs for credit and greater freedom in marketing. Merchant credit in general is expensive and unsatisfactory and its use should be still further reduced.

FARM LABOR AND EQUIPMENT

The present tendency toward increased employment in industry, road building, and construction work points to a stronger competition for farm labor during the spring and summer of 1925 than prevailed during 1924. Somewhat higher wages will probably be paid farm labor as a result. From present indications little change in farm equipment and upkeep costs for the country as a whole are to be expected.

Farm wages were higher in July, 1924, in the South and Southwestern States than in July, 1923, and lower at that time over the remainder of the country. During the latter part of the summer of 1924, the improved conditions of the spring wheat farmers and the demand for harvest labor brought wages in North and South Dakota and Minnesota to levels higher than a year previous, while most of the Southern States held to the wage levels established in July.

The cost of farm equipment and upkeep has been increasing since the low point of 1922 when retail prices of representative items purchased by farmers were between 60 and 70 per cent higher than pre-war prices. In November, 1924, prices of farm machinery and other materials averaged between 75 and 80 per cent above pre-war prices. Recent reports from the farm implement industry, however, indicate slight reductions in wholesale prices and increased sales.

No marked change in farm equipment and upkeep costs is to be expected however, during the present year, and, with the present upward tendency in farm wages, both labor and equipment costs during the summer of 1925 will be about the same level—something like 75 per cent above the pre-war averages of 1910–1914.

WHEAT

If there is an average world crop of wheat in 1925, the present high prices of wheat can not be expected to prevail for the 1925 crop, although prices are expected to be better than in 1923. Growers of hard spring wheat are cautioned not to increase production above domestic requirements. If the spring wheat acreage in the United States is held to that of last year and an average yield is secured, the production of hard spring wheat should about equal domestic requirements.

The year 1924 witnessed the very unusual situation of a large United States crop of wheat coming at a time of short world crop. The result was that the wheat grower in this country with a larger crop than in 1923 realized a much higher price per bushel than he received for the smaller crop of the year before. Present prices should not lead wheat farmers to deviate from programs looking toward a balanced system of agriculture.

The short crop of the world was due chiefly to low yields outside of the United States, and only slightly to a smaller acreage. The greatest decrease in production occurred in Canada, with considerable decreases in Argentina, Italy, and Germany. The prevailing high price of wheat, as compared with the price for several years past, is due not alone to a 10 per cent reduction in the world crop, but also to an increase in the world demand, which since 1918 has been on a definitely lower level than it was before the war. The low price that prevailed last year up to midsummer, due primarily to the large 1923 crop and heavy stocks, stimulated foreign consumption.

It appears that the world supplies at the beginning of the harvest of this year's crop will be very low. A small carry over will be a strengthening factor in the market until the movement of the new crop gets well under way, and should help maintain prices for the early crop, but the world's wheat acreage and the developments in the condition of the 1925 crop will determine the market trend and ultimately the price.

The winter wheat acreage sown for the crop that will come onto the market this year, as reported for the United States, Canada, India, and eight European countries, shows an increase of about 3½ per cent over that of last year. The total acreage reported for winter wheat represents more than half of the total winter and spring wheat area of the Northern Hemisphere outside of Russia and China. The European countries reporting, which represent more than half of the total wheat acreage of Europe, show a slight decrease. If the plantings in other European countries have shown no increase, the winter wheat acreage in the Northern Hemisphere is still somewhat larger than last year, and barring serious winter killing and unfavorable weather during the growing season should produce a crop of winter wheat equal to that of 1923. The condition of winter wheat in the United States and western Europe is generally reported as good, but conditions are less favorable in the important wheat section of the lower Danube Basin.

Canada will begin the season next spring under somewhat of a handicap, for the fall plowing of land intended for next year's crop is reported as only 32 per cent, as compared with 43 per cent last year and 48 per cent in the

Durum wheat will probably be less profitable than hard spring wheat except in those regions where higher yields are generally secured. A short crop of durum wheat in the Mediterranean Basin and an increasing demand in this country have recently forced prices for this class of wheat to a level nearly as high as that for hard spring. The prices of durum wheat depend largely upon the export demand, since the production in this country is larger than our consumption. There has been some increase in the competition with durum wheat in the foreign markets by hard wheat from Canada and North Africa. If an average crop is secured in foreign countries, it may be expected to reduce the export demand for our durum; and a continuation of the present high price of durum as compared with hard red spring wheat could not be expected.

RYE

A review of the rye situation is necessary in considering the outlook for wheat since rye is an important competitor of wheat in many European markets. The shortage in the world's rye crop last year not only caused high prices for the rye produced in the United States, but has also contributed to the high prices of wheat. The rye acreage sown for next year's harvest in 12 countries reporting to date shows an increase of 5 per cent over last year's acreage. These countries last year had more than half of the world's total rye acreage outside of Russia. The area sown in the 10 European countries reporting to date is 6 per cent greater than last year's area in the same countries. No report has yet been received as to the acreage sown to rye in Germany which is the largest rye producer in the world outside of Russia. The condition of the winter rye seedings in Germany is reported to be above average.

The rye crop outside of Russia was 16 per cent or 149,000,000 bushels below the crop of 1923. Moreover, last year Russia contributed 35,000,000 bushels to the supply outside of Russia, whereas this year she will contribute nothing. Such a shortage is not to be expected from next year's harvest.

FLAX

Seed flax acreage may still be increased somewhat before production with average yields will equal the present consumptive demand. It seems probable that flaxseed prices in the United States will be on a relatively higher level than wheat during the next crop year if production is below the domestic requirements.

Some margin must be allowed between production and consumption needs to make the full amount of the duty effective but from the best information available it appears that the present active demand for flaxseed is likely to continue during the next crop year and that it will be sufficient to absorb a material increase over this year's production without placing United States flax on an export basis.

The flax acreage has been increased between 800,000 and 900,000 acres each year since 1922 and flaxseed production in 1924, totaling slightly over 30,000,000 bushels, was the largest on record. But increased building and repainting, which had been neglected during the war, together with improving financial conditions, have caused increased demand for oil with resulting advance in prices.

During the war period, flax acreage was reduced in favor of wheat until production was brought down to around 12,000,000 bushels. Exports were almost negligible while imports exceeded yearly production by about 2,000,000 bushels.

Acreage in 1921 was still smaller than during the war period, totaling but little over a million acres. Because of the general business depression, however, prices declined to about $1.45 per bushel, as the average farm price and imports were decreased until the total supply of flaxseed in the United States for that year was only 21,650,000 bushels.

In 1922 production and net imports totaled 38,243,000 bushels and in 1923 about 37,438,000 bushels. According to the best information available the linseed-oil requirements of the United States for 1924–25 will be the equivalent of about 40,000,000 bushels of flaxseed.

Since 1921 world production has increased about 55,000,000 bushels. If world production is increased further during 1925, flax prices likely will be lower than at present.

COTTON

The outlook for cotton production in 1925, though perhaps less favorable than 1924 from the standpoint of production costs, is otherwise encouraging. From present indications stocks at the end of the current season will not be large, foreign demand should be sustained, industry is in a liquidated condition, and cotton growers in general are in an improved financial position. It appears that the world could absorb at sustained prices a crop of 12 to 13 million bales and that producers in those sections of the belt where conditions are favorable for cotton production at present prices would be justified in planting not to exceed their 1924 acreage.

It now appears probable that the consumption of American cotton during the season 1924–25 will be considerably greater than that of last season and that although the carry over at the end of this season will be somewhat in excess of that from the 1923–24 crop, it will not be burdensome.

From the movement of the 1924 crop it may be inferred that the present season's supply of American cotton will be well enough digested to permit easy distribution of the 1925 crop. Exports to date have been much heavier than last year. European purchasers have been buying freely and there is greater activity in the cotton mills in England and Germany than at this time last year. The stabilization of exchange has made it possible for European merchants to participate to a larger extent in the handling of the crops, and stocks in European ports which have for the past three years been abnormally low are now increasing. On the other hand, although mills in Great Britain have slightly increased the number of working hours per week over last year, they are still on a short-time schedule with but little increase in exports of cotton goods. United States exports of raw cotton to France, Italy, and Japan are substantially greater than last year.

Offsetting the strength in the export movement was the low consumption of American mills in the early fall compared with the fall of 1923. But on the other hand, the American industry seems to be fully liquidated, stocks of manufactured goods being much less throughout the industry, so far as ascertainable at this time, than in the fall of 1923. Mill stocks of raw cotton are also less than last year. Consequently any increase in consumer demand would be likely to be felt promptly in the movement of raw cotton. The sections of this report on "foreign and domestic demand" show that a sustained if not increased demand, especially in the United States, is probable, indicating that the season's large crop will be well absorbed.

A survey of the foreign growths shows an unusually large production in India this season. Most Indian cotton, being of shorter length, does not ordinarily compete directly with the American crop except when the price of American cotton is relatively high, but the general effect of an increased supply of Indian cotton can not be ignored. It should be noted, incidentally, that there is an increasing area in India in which varieties which do compete directly are being grown, though it will probably be some years before the tendency toward better staples will offer serious competition. The Egyptian crop is larger this year, but not unusually large. Material increase of production in Egypt is unlikely. In other countries, notwithstanding the continued effort to encourage cotton growing, the total production is not a large factor in the world market. No very good figures of world carry over of all cotton can be obtained at this time. Such information as is available indicates that the world carry over will be somewhat larger than for either of the two preceding years but not excessively so.

Looking at the conditions under which the 1925 crop will be produced it is apparent that although the present crop was of about the same value as that of the last year it was produced more uniformly throughout the belt than in the two preceding seasons. As a result, financial conditions in the Cotton Belt have materially improved, particularly in regions that have escaped the boll weevil. Banking conditions are good, and interest rates are lower. Present indications are that the 1925–26 cotton crop will be produced at a slightly higher cost per acre than the two preceding crops. The trend of wages paid to farm labor is slightly upward, especially in Texas, Oklahoma, North Carolina, and Alabama, where competition with industries is most noticeable. The cost of keeping mules will be appreciably higher because of higher feed prices. Wholesale prices of materials used in the manufacture of fertilizers indicate that cotton fertilizers will cost the farmer slightly more than last year. These three items of cost roughly approximate two-thirds of the total cost of production, taking the belt as a whole.

On the other hand, there are a few costs that in many regions have a tendency toward lower levels, such as farm machinery, planting seed, and calcium arsenate. Calcium arsenate, from present indications, will be available at the lowest price prevailing since it has been recommended for weevil control. Individual growers should estimate the minimum amount they will need and secure that amount during the early spring. By doing so farmers not only save money by avoiding the higher prices forced by rush demands on limited local supplies, but also will make it possible for manufacturers to stabilize their production and provide an adequate supply.

In addition to a general tendency for slightly higher costs for growing an acre of cotton in 1925, it is likely that there will be an even greater increase in the cost of growing a pound of cotton as compared with 1924. This is based on the assumption that there is a greater chance that yields will be less in 1925 as compared with 1924 than the chance of their being greater, since 1924 witnessed unusually high yields. Low yields, however, with accompanying lower production would probably result in a price that would offset the increased cost per pound.

In summary it appears that, assuming a continuance of business prosperity and barring unusual developments, the world could absorb at sustained prices a crop of American cotton in 1925–26 of twelve to thirteen million bales. However, in the event that the producers of cotton respond to prices of the pre-planting season in the same manner that they have for the past 10 years, there will be a decrease in acreage, although the better financial conditions in the belt, with producers in position to finance a full acreage, will tend to offset this usual tendency. In the event that this should prove to be the case, and assuming lower yields, the 1925–26 crop will be somewhat less than the 1924–25, hence would be absorbed at sustained or higher prices. It must be remembered, however, that the effect of the growing season's weather can not be foretold—good weather would mean another high yield.

In shaping their program for 1925 growers should, of course, consider carefully local conditions in connection with the more general situation, and the prospects for a profitable employment of their land, labor, and equipment in the production of other crops, particularly in the production of feed.

HOGS

Hog producers enter 1925 with 18 per cent fewer hogs than a year ago and every indication that prices during the next 18 months will be higher than at any time since 1920. Six to eight million fewer pigs will be born next spring than last spring. Fewer sows will farrow next fall than farrowed last fall if producers respond to the unfavorable relation of corn and hog prices as they have done in the past. Nevertheless, conditions are favorable for expanding fall farrowing. Breeding plans should be based not on present price relations, but on the relations that are expected to prevail when the pigs are ready for market.

A further reduction in hog production is highly undesirable both from the point of view of requirements for domestic consumers and from that of long-time policy of production.

Compared to the trend in the slaughter of hogs, the pigs born during 1924 represented about a normal crop. The reduction to normal has already caused hog prices to rise to about the equivalent of the average price for the period 1909–1913, taking account of the change in the purchasing power of money. Farmers' reports of sows bred or to be bred for spring farrowing indicate that the spring crop of pigs in the Corn Belt will be about 25 to 27 million, as compared to 33 million in 1924 and 40 million in 1923. This will result in receipts in the fall and winter of 1925–26 much lighter than for several years.

The present business situation indicates that during 1925 American demand will be at least as active as during 1924. The foreign outlook is for steady demand, the improved purchasing power of Germany and the gradually improving economic conditions in other countries enabling them to continue as active bidders for pork and lard. However, still higher prices will undoubtedly result in decreases in the volume of our pork and lard exports.

Present supply and demand conditions are sufficient to assure a year of prices higher than in any recent period except that of war-time inflation.

If the recent high price of corn stimulates some increase in acreage, even with a yield per acre as low as that of 1924, the total production would be somewhat greater in 1925. The number of livestock has been so greatly decreased since a year ago that even an average yield of corn would prove more than enough for all ordinary feeding demands. Should there be a large yield of corn, with the reduced demand, considerably lower corn prices would result.

These facts indicate that the chances are in favor of fall pigs proving profitable enough to justify some expansion in sows bred for fall farrowing above the number of last year. Fall farrowings may be materially increased by breeding gilts for early fall farrowing that might otherwise be sent to market. It is probable that prices will be good for sows next winter. In fact, the full force of the shortage of hogs will probably not be felt in the markets until the early part of the run of 1925-26 or later, depending upon the size of the 1925 corn crop.

The shortage of the hogs for 1925-26 offers the South an opportunity to supply a large part of its own demand for pork in a year when prices will be attractive. The extent to which hog production in the South may be profitably expanded depends largely upon the extent to which the production of feed crops can be increased. Where peanuts or more corn can be grown in 1925 it probably will pay to expand farrowing in the fall of 1925 up to the limit of the available feed.

CORN

The 1924 corn crop will probably be well cleaned up, but an increased acreage in 1925 does not appear advisable in view of the indicated reduction in the feeding demand. Stocks of old corn on farms are likely to be smaller than usual in the beginning of the new crop year 1925, but it appears that not more than an average crop will be required to supply the needs of the country for both feed and commercial purposes.

Acreage as large as that planted in 1924, if coupled with yields as large as in recent years, except 1924, would produce a crop in excess of the probable feeding demand and other domestic requirements and result in materially lower prices to farmers who sell all their corn.

The prospect for a large corn crop in 1924 indicated by slightly increased plantings failed to materialize because of adverse weather conditions, and the total production fell short of the 1923 crop by more than 600,000,000 bushels. The carry over from the 1923 crop was not large, so that the prospect of a much smaller supply of corn this year resulted in a rapid advance in prices.

This advance in price, together with the decreased feeding demand on farms, has caused a heavier marketing of corn than was expected, and commercial stocks have been materially increased. The reduction in the number of cattle and hogs on feed will result in a reduction of between 350,000,000 and 400,000,000 bushels in feed requirements during the present crop year. Other feed grains, the total supply of which is about 235,000,000 bushels larger than last year, and which have been relatively cheaper than corn, are also being used extensively to supplement the short crop.

The higher prices have caused the most economical feeding of corn, and it appears that the feeding requirements are being rapidly adjusted to the supply so that sufficient corn will be available for commercial needs and allow for some carry over into the next crop year. The poor quality of the crop in a large section of the Corn Belt, however, will reduce the effective supply considerably below the amount indicated by the production figures. With the smallest hog production during the past 10 years indicated, and with no material increases contemplated in the number of cattle or other livestock, the domestic feeding demand will be materially smaller for the 1925 crop than during the present crop year.

Farmers who will need corn early in the fall should plant an early maturing variety for at least a portion of the crop to supply these needs.

BEEF CATTLE

Prices for beef cattle in 1925 should average somewhat higher than for 1924. The industry is gradually working into a more favorable position due to the relation of beef to competing commodities, especially pork, and to improved industrial conditions, and in no small measure to the cattleman's own sacrifices. Market receipts will probably be somewhat smaller than in 1924. All conditions indicate that the long-time outlook for the industry is even more favorable. In a word, the sun of hope for the cattleman seems to be in sight, but it is still on the horizon, and will probably not reach the zenith until several years hence.

For the next few months reductions in the number of cattle at markets will be confined largely to better grades or, in other words, to grain-finished cattle. Lower grades will be plentiful and the supply is expected to meet increased competition from dairy cattle. Presumably the price spread between the better grades of grain-finished cattle and the lower grades will lessen in seasonal manner during the next few months and then widen materially as the year advances. With any improvement in the feed situation and in the prospective prices for fed cattle, a fairly active demand for stockers and feeders is expected in the fall of 1925, and prices on such cattle should average a little higher than in the fall of 1924.

As a war legacy the beef cattle industry has been suffering from overproduction during the last five years. The domestic demand has not been sufficient to consume the quantity of beef produced at prices remunerative to the cattleman. The trend to a more normal production has been evidenced by a marked shift from beef cattle to dairying and to sheep, particularly during the last two years. Some of the most pronounced signs of liquidation were evident during the past year. As compared with 1923, nearly 600,000 fewer cattle and calves were returned from market centers to the country for finishing, although receipts were the largest since 1919. This resulted in an increase of 6.3 per cent in the number of cattle and calves slaughtered over 1923.

The stocker and feeder movement at all markets during the last six months of 1924, compared with 1923, showed a decrease of 14 per cent. The estimate of cattle on feed in the Corn Belt on January 1, 1925, showed a decrease of 18 per cent, compared with January 1, 1924. Marketing and slaughter in December were the largest for that month since 1919. While feeding cattle were bought lower than in 1923, this small saving has been, in many instances, discounted by high feed costs. The high cost of feed will no doubt shorten feeding periods, thus limiting the number of well-finished cattle for the summer and fall markets.

The estimated number of cattle other than milk cows on farms and ranges January 1, 1925, was 39,609,000, compared with 41,720,000 in 1924. The estimated number in 12 range States declined 4.6 per cent from last year, and is 7.9 per cent below 1922, indicating a continued downward trend in range cattle production.

Physical conditions in the range States during the last half of 1924 were generally the poorest since the disastrous year of 1919. Fall and winter ranges were generally poor to bad. Hay and forage crops were short and prices high. Since the middle of the summer the drought condition has extended to the large areas in the Southwest. On January 1 the condition of ranges was 77 compared with 91 for last year. Condition of cattle was 84 compared with 93 for January 1 last year. Already considerable losses have been reported and the 1925 calf crop will doubtless be below the average for the last four years.

Liquidation of old range cattle loans continues. The balance due the War Finance Corporation by livestock loan companies on November 30, 1924, was 21.9 per cent of the amount originally advanced to all livestock loan companies. Old loans made by private agencies have been greatly reduced. Credit for new range cattle loans is limited and should be used to improve the herd rather than increase its numbers.

Even at present price levels, American beef can not compete with Argentine beef in European markets, so there is no prospect of an improved export trade. On the other hand any probable increase in the price level is not likely to be great enough to attract Argentine beef to the United States.

While industrial conditions are expected to continue favorable, the greatest strength in the beef market will be due to the decreased supply of pork products. The price situation has changed materially during the last six months and consumers' demand is expected to shift more to beef as the supply of pork diminishes.

DAIRYING

Further expansion in dairying in 1925 seems inadvisable. A recovery in prices of dairy products could hardly be expected should the number of milk cows be further increased. In addition to the fact that domestic production appears adequate, the foreign dairy situation is such as to keep world market prices low and thus limit the height to which our butter prices can rise without bringing in foreign butter.

The marked expansion of dairying in the principal butter sections shown by the increase of 4.2 per cent in the estimated number of milk cows in that area during 1924 as compared to a 2.2 per cent increase for the whole county, was largely caused by the unfavorable returns from other farm enterprises since the war.

Beginning the year 1924 with an increase in estimated number of milk cows on farms of but 1.4 per cent over January 1, 1923, production increased fully 3 per cent during 1924, because of the unusually favorable weather and pasture conditions during the flush season, resulting in the low butter prices which prevailed the second half of the year. With most of this increase in production diverted into butter, production of butter increased approximately 8 per cent over 1923. This heavy production was reflected in the accumulation of stocks in storage which on September 1 reached a peak of 156,440,000 pounds. Under the influence of these conditions butter prices did not follow the usual upward tendency during the late summer and early fall months.

Domestic consumption should continue heavy in 1925 as favorable industrial conditions throughout most of the year are expected, and because of the tendency toward heavier per capita consumption of milk and dairy products stimulated by advertising and educational work.

European demand for dairy products can not be expected to improve in the near future as it did during the past year. The United Kingdom is now consuming more heavily than in pre-war years. Germany is already fully back to pre-war volume of butter imports. The recovery of imports in that country took place within the past year, exerting an unusually strengthening influence upon world markets and offsetting the effect of heavier world production. Russia is an increasingly important source of supply for the world's markets. Countries in the Southern Hemisphere, including New Zealand, Australia, and Argentine, where dairy production is now exceeding all previous records, are to be regarded as important influences in the world's butter markets during the coming year and probably as increasingly important influences in the future.

While 1924 may not have been as profitable a year for dairying generally as was 1923, those who have recently gone into the dairy business would do well not to abandon it because of a single year of higher returns from other farm enterprises. Weeding out the least efficient cows and feeding more carefully would help to meet the present situation, and still leave the farmers of the country in good position to meet the steady growth in the demand for dairy products which each year is showing.

SHEEP AND WOOL

Prospects for the sheep industry in 1925 appear favorable. The world outlook and the prospective meat situation in this country promise prices for 1925 at least on a par with those of 1924. There does not appear to be any immediate danger of overproduction, as the increase in the number of sheep has as yet been only slight.

For more than two years lambs and wool have commanded prices well above those of most farm products and more than 50 per cent above the pre-war level. After 1925 some recession in returns from sheep may occur.

Market receipts of sheep and lambs may show a moderate increase over those of 1924, but with somewhat better demand it is not anticipated that this increase will be sufficiently large to bring about any marked lowering of the average price but frequent and wide temporary and seasonal fluctuations in price are anticipated.

During 1924, wool advanced sharply with increasing consumption and the disappearance of the war accumulations. American wool prices are ordinarily closely related to world prices, since more than half of all our wool is imported though a large portion of our requirements of certain grades are produced here.

With low business activity, American mills consumed about one-sixth less wool in 1924 than in 1923. There has been a decided increase in activity since the middle of 1924, and with expected further improvement in business activity it seems probable that the demand for wool during 1925 will be stronger than during 1924. Our wool prices are still somewhat below the world level, taking account of the tariff, and with increasing domestic consumption further advances may occur.

Some expansion has been going on in the industry ever since the low point of production was reached in 1922. Thus far this expansion has not materially affected market receipts, which in 1924 were only 175,000 head greater than in 1923. This may mean that animals were kept at home to increase the breeding stock instead of being sent to market. However, the 2 per cent increase in the estimated number of sheep this January over last January does not indicate that the expansion has yet been great.

During the past year or two there has been a rather marked tendency for cattlemen to shift to sheep, and if this movement continues for a time it will materially increase and hasten expansion in the sheep industry.

There has been some expansion of sheep in the spring-wheat country. On farms in these sections and in other sections where there is a definite place for a flock of sheep, even with materially lower prices for lambs, they may be profitable, but this should not be interpreted as a recommendation that sheep be introduced on those farms where they can not ordinarily compete with hogs and cattle.

HORSES AND MULES

Though there are as many horses and mules of working age on farms as will be needed for the coming season, a decided decline in colt production during the past few years points to a future shortage of good work stock. This shortage is likely to be acute during the time that colts foaled this year and next, and even young horses purchased now, are still in active service.

To prevent a shortage of good farm work stock a few years hence there might well be a somewhat larger number of mares bred in 1925 than in 1924 on farms where there are good mares that can be bred to good stallions or jacks.

On January 1, 1925, the number of horses and mules on farms in the United States was about 91 per cent of the number on farms in 1920. During this time colt production fell off decidedly, indicating that a large part of the decrease was in the number of young animals. Reports from 32 States show that in 1920 the number of colts foaled per 1,000 head of all horses and mules on farms at the end of the year was about 92 per cent of the number foaled in 1919; in 1921, 80 per cent; in 1922, 67 per cent; in 1923, 53 per cent; and in 1924, only 50 per cent. In 1924 the general downward tendency to colt production was checked decidedly, indicating that farmers in some areas are beginning to realize a need for younger horses to replace the older ones now in use.

By the time the present supply is so short as to cause an upward change in horse prices there is likely to be a considerable shortage of young animals. Any attempt to overcome this shortage at a late date would accentuate the shortage of work stock because large numbers of mares would be bred and could not then do a full year's work.

While the primary reason for the decline in the price of horses, which began in 1911, was overproduction, undoubtedly this decline was accentuated because of the increasing use of trucks, automobiles, and tractors. Also, it is believed that there has been a general let-up in breeding for high-grade animals, and that at present a relatively large proportion of farm horses and mules are not only old but of an inferior quality.

POULTRY

The outlook of the poultry industry during 1925 from the standpoint of market egg prices is favorable, while from the standpoint of immediate market poultry prices it is not as encouraging. It seems probable that higher egg prices will prevail during the season of flush production this year than last. With an abnormally large stock of dressed poultry in storage it seems probable that lower prices on market poultry may prevail for at least the first half of the year. However, higher prices for other meats should have a strengthening effect upon poultry prices during the latter part of 1925 and the early months of 1926, which, coupled with probable reduced feed costs, should make that period a more profitable one.

The laying stock of chickens now on farms must produce the egg crop of the coming spring and summer and its output can be supplemented toward the close of the year only to a limited extent by the pullets hatched in 1925. Egg receipts at the principal markets during 1924 were decidedly below 1923. This decrease in receipts persisted through the fall and winter to the end of January. With a 9 per cent decrease in the number of poultry on farms on January 1, 1925, compared with a year ago, there is reason to suppose that the egg crop of this year will not exceed that of the last year.

. The storage-egg business last year was very profitable. . Storage-egg stocks, both shell and frozen, at the beginning of this year were well below those on January 1, 1924, and slightly below the five-year average. These facts, together with present good prices and an indicated crop of moderate size should result in a higher price level during the storage season and a favorable price level during the remainder of the year.

The present poultry disease epidemic complicates the situation to some extent. If the epidemic is controlled in the near future, as seems probable, it will have little effect upon either the egg or poultry crop of 1925.

Present high feed costs on commercial egg farms and the shortage of corn which exists in sections of the Middle West may also affect egg production unfavorably owing to a less liberal feeding policy.

The immediate outlook for poultry is less favorable. The disease epidemic has seriously interfered with the movement to market live poultry and has resulted in a decreased demand for both live and dressed poultry. As a result, prices paid to producers have declined materially in many sections, while the stocks of dressed poultry in storage have mounted rapidly, reaching a total on January 1, 1925, of over 133,500,000 pounds, the largest holdings ever recorded.

The consumption of poultry must increase somewhat in order to move these stocks out of storage. To effect this increase in consumption, lower prices appear inevitable, unless meat prices in general increase, thus making poultry relatively more economical as food.

OATS

Oats production in 1924 was slightly in excess of domestic requirements, and with no increase probable in domestic consumption during the next crop year, any increase in the oats acreage in 1925 does not seem advisable.

Exports from the 1924 crop totaled only about 4,000,000 bushels to January 1, 1925, with no indications at this time of any material improvement in the export demand. Without an important export outlet the oats crop must be utilized largely on the farms.

Scarcity and high price of corn this year is no doubt increasing the use of oats as feed for horses and for dairy cattle, sheep, and young stock; but there are nearly 3,500,000 fewer horses and mules on farms than five years ago, while the number of other livestock on farms has also been slightly decreased.

Receipts at the principal markets for the crop year to date have been about 24 per cent larger than for the corresponding period during the past two years and commercial stocks have reached nearly 75,000,000 bushels, the largest amount on record.

. The large supply of oats is causing prices of this grain to lag behind the prices of other grains. Prices are slightly higher than last year, but the advance has been caused almost entirely by the high corn prices. Had the corn crop equaled the five-year average it is probable that the 1924 crop of oats would have sold below the 1923 prices.

BARLEY

Barley prices are at relatively high levels because of a sharp decrease in the world's production and the high price of other feed grains, but the general situation suggests that last year's acreage was sufficient under normal conditions to produce sufficient barley for domestic requirements and for the limited export demand for malting barley.

European production was materially smaller than normal in 1924, and the quality of the crop was damaged somewhat by rain. This increased the export demand in the United States. A larger percentage than normal of the current year's exports has been drawn from the North Central States because of the relatively larger crop in these States and the small crops on the Pacific coast.

During the past five years market receipts have been less than half as large as formerly, notwithstanding that production has been maintained, which indicates increased farm feeding, but it is probable that with the sharp reduction in hog production the feeding demand may be materially smaller next year unless there should be a small crop of feed grains.

In those sections where corn is short and feed grains will be urgently needed early in the season sufficient barley to meet these needs might be very advantageous, but an analysis of the general situation suggests that the 1924 acreage in the United States except on the Pacific coast should produce as much as wil be needed for the domestic feeding demand.

On the Pacific coast acreage should probably be brought back to that of 1923 as a fairly steady demand prevails for barley in that territory.

HAY

The relatively lower level of timothy hay prices at this time compared with last year suggests that the production of market hay should be more closely adjusted to the decreasing demand. Dairy hay has held firm, particularly alfalfa, and a general survey of the situation indicates that production might be increased profitably where the local supply is not equal to the consumption.

With the record crop in 1924, hay prices with the exception of those for alfalfa, declined close to the level of the heavy 1922 crop. Even at the reduced prices offerings were ample for market needs and it was apparent that country holdings were large so that any advance in prices would call out increased shipments.

The 76,034,000 acres of hay harvested in 1924 represented an increase of 0.2 per cent over the 1923 acreage while the yield of 1.44 tons per acre was only slightly larger than the 1923 production of 1.41 tons which equalled the 10-year average. Given normal yields it appears that this acreage is sufficient for balanced production.

The tendency is toward a greater degree of self-sufficiency in forage production as evidenced by an increasing acreage of tame hay in many of the Southern States and by a greater acreage of alfalfa in the North Central States. Market reports indicate that some few territories which formerly purchased alfalfa now have a small surplus for shipment. It is obvious that unless the total production is to be increased this increase in consuming territory must be balanced by a corresponding decrease in the surplus-producing sections. High freight rates may make it inadvisable to attempt to produce for more than local needs in territories remote from market.

FEEDSTUFFS AND FEED CROPS

Supply of feedstuffs and forage, including grains, high protein concentrates, and manufactured feeds is apparently sufficient until the new feed crops become available, and the price trend based on approximately normal conditions is more likely to work downward than upward.

The 1924 hay crop was the largest on record. A large part of the increase was in timothy territory and timothy prices will probably remain below last year. The supply of alfalfa, clover, and other legumes appears to be adequate at practically last year's prices until the new crop is available.

It seems probable that the consuming demand for feed grains for this period will not equal that of 1924. The use of feed grains, which depends largely upon the number of domestic animals available to consume such feedstuffs is considerably influenced by available supplies of high protein concentrates. A substantial decrease in the number of hogs is assured. The number of beef cattle has also decreased materially, while there has been only a slight increase in the number of sheep and dairy animals. As feed grains are at present quoted relatively higher in most sections than are the high protein concentrates the increased use of commercial feeds will lead to a corresponding decrease in the amount of grains fed. Furthermore, it is likely that the demand for prepared feeds, and feed grains from the poultry trade will be less than it was during 1924 owing to a less liberal feeding policy and smaller numbers of poultry on farms.

The supply of barley is limited and prices have advanced because of an active export demand and the high price of corn. Less barley is available for feed than a year ago, and the supply will no doubt be largely consumed before the new crop is available.

Despite the very large decrease, approximately 600,000,000 bushels, in the corn crop and the apparently unsatisfactory condition of pastures in Western and Southwestern States, these factors will be largely offset by the availability of other grains and feeds and by the increase in the last hay crop.

POTATOES

The present price of potatoes is likely to result in too small an acreage of potatoes this year. Many growers, including even some who are producing potatoes at a low cost per bushel, have been unduly discouraged by the ruinous prices which were paid in many localities for much of the 1924 crop. Such growers should bear in mind that much less than the usual acreage of potatoes was grown in 1924, and that the exceptionally heavy production was largely the result of remarkably favorable weather. On the other hand, the planting of such a large acreage of potatoes as that of 1922 would be a great mistake, for although a yield per acre as heavy as that of 1924 may not be secured again for a number of years, there is reason to expect future yields to average substantially higher than they have in the past. This means that the needs of the country can be met with fewer acres of potatoes per thousand of population. In the South, however, the increasing yield per acre is less of a problem this season than is the prospect of competing with the low-priced potatoes now on the Northern markets.

Potato growing is in a state of transition. A steadily increasing proportion of the potatoes raised for sale is being produced by those growers who have an acreage large enough to justify the use of improved machinery for cultivating, spraying, digging, and grading the crop. A growing proportion of the acreage is being planted in those sections where the average yield is high. A greater emphasis than formerly is being placed on seed improvement, seed treatment, and the use of fertilizers. The better quality of product, the increased yields secured and the use of improved equipment are together increasing the number of bushels of marketable potatoes which the larger growers can produce with a given amount of labor. The more efficient growers are reducing the cost of production. In the long run this will reduce the profits of those growers who raise potatoes for sale in quantities too small to justify the purchase of efficient equipment.

An example of the changes taking place in the method of growing potatoes is the fact that the quantity of seed potatoes certified by public agencies as suitable for seed has increased to nearly six times the quantity certified three years ago. There is now sufficient certified seed to plant nearly a fifth of the entire acreage. In addition, a very large quantity of seed potatoes grown from stock certified in 1923 is available. This represents an advance in the average quality of potatoes used for seed which has no parallel in the case of any other important crop in this country.

In 1924 less than the usual number of acres were planted to potatoes, the acreage being 4 per cent less than in 1923 and 15 per cent below the very large acreage grown in 1922. If the yield per acre in 1924 had been only 99 bushels, or the same as the average of the previous 10 years (1914–1923), the production would have been an average of only 3.2 bushels per person in the United States, or 15 per cent less than the 20-year average per capita production. The yield in 1924 was, however, 124.2 bushels per acre, 25 bushels per acre above the previous 10-year average and 11 bushels per acre above the largest yield previously secured in the United States as a whole.

During the last 30 years the average yield of potatoes in the United States has been increasing at an average rate of nearly a bushel per acre each year. Additional allowance must now be made for the effect on yields of the great improvement in the average quality of the seed potatoes used. It therefore appears that if in 1925 weather conditions are about as favorable to potatoes as they are in an average year, the yield per acre may reach, say 108 or 110 bushels per acre, instead of 100.6 bushels, the average of the last 10 years, including the heavy yield of 1924. If the higher of these yields is secured this season an acreage even 5 per cent larger than the reduced acreage of 1924 would produce the usual quantity of potatoes per capita.

There are many local variations in the potato outlook. During the war when the prices of farm products were high in proportion to freight rates, potato production was greatly stimulated in some States remote from the principal markets. The acreage of potatoes in the five States of Minnesota, North Dakota, South Dakota, Colorado, and Idaho increased from less than 500,000 acres in 1914 to over 1,000,000 acres in 1922. Since then overproduction and low prices, combined with higher freight rates, have caused the acreage in these States to decline. In 1924 only 700,000 acres were grown and yet the price there has been so low that millions of bushels have been fed to livestock and in the Dakotas a considerable acreage was left undug. Growers in these States should watch closely the acreage planted elsewhere because in recent years of overproduction they have been the ones who suffered the most.

SWEET POTATOES

Present high prices for sweet potatoes should not influence growers to plant a largely increased acreage of this crop this year. Present prices are due more to low yields in 1924 than to short acreage. An increase of more than 10 per cent over 1924 acreage with an average yield is likely to produce more than can be marketed profitably.

The trend of per capita production of sweet potatoes has been markedly upward. It has increased from the pre-war average of 0.6 bushels to an average of 0.94 bushels for the 5-year period previous to 1924. In 1922, when the crop averaged slightly more than 1 bushel per person for the entire population of the United States, the high point of profitable production per capita was passed, for prices dropped so low that the acreage the next year was sharply reduced. On the other hand, the extent to which the demand for this crop is increasing is shown by the fact that in a number of the Southern States the price for the 1924 crop was the highest on record, notwithstanding the fact that the per capita production in the United States was nearly 8 per cent above the pre-war average. Probably under present conditions production can be increased to about 0.95 bushel per capita before sweet potatoes become less profitable, on the average, than competing crops.

The increased consumption of sweet potatoes is due partially to the fact that the consuming season has been lengthened and losses in storage reduced by the development of improved methods of curing and storing the crop, and partially, as with vegetables generally, to the higher standard of living of a large part of the population. The ideal for growers as a whole should be, therefore, to maintain such a moderate and uniform production from season to season that prices to growers will be reasonably profitable and yet the price to consumers sufficiently low to maintain and, if possible, to increase further the per capita consumption of this crop.

Much of the increase in production during the last 10 years has been in the southern districts, where the bulk of the crop is consumed locally and where farmers have found it desirable to substitute sweet potatoes on some of their former cotton acreage. The increase has been shared by the commercial sections which ship to northern markets.

There are some local variations in the outlook for sweet potatoes. In the Cotton Belt, where moist-fleshed varieties, such as the Nancy Hall, are grown and preferred, the price has been particularly high this season and it is there that an excessive acreage in 1925 is most to be feared. In the commercial sweet potato region that extends from the Eastern Shore of Virginia into New Jersey, the northern or Jersey type of sweet potato is grown for shipment to northern markets. This region has less than 10 per cent of the total acreage of sweet potatoes in the United States but ships about two-thirds of those that move by rail. Growers in this section raised the usual number of acres of sweet potatoes in 1924, had a fair yield and secured high prices. In planning their 1925 acreage they should not overlook the fact that the present high prices are, in part, the result of the very short crop of sweet potatoes in the States further South.

PEANUTS

Any substantial increase in peanut acreage in 1925 over that of last year may result in lower prices. It would appear that the 1925 acreages of both the large-podded Virginia type and of the small-podded Spanish and Runner types should not be appreciably increased but may remain fairly safely at the present levels. However, the present price level for Spanish and Runner types is not as satisfactory as for the Virginia type and there is danger of further price reductions if acreage is increased.

Although the recent trend of production of the Spanish and Runner types which are produced principally in Georgia, Alabama, Florida, and South Carolina, and to a lesser extent in Texas, Oklahoma, and Arkansas, has been downward, the 1924 crop was 16 per cent larger than that of the preceding year. This was due to an increase in both acreage and yield per acre. Quality was poorer, however, and a larger proportion than normal has been sold to oil mills.

Imports do not materially affect the situation with regard to these varieties, as imported peanuts are almost entirely of the Virginia type. There is no reason to suppose that domestic demand will increase to any great extent during the next year and therefore any substantial increase in production will under normal conditions result in considerably lower prices. Growers generally agree that present prices can not be lowered appreciably without wiping out whatever margin of profit now exists.

Consumption of Virginia-type peanuts for the crop year ending November 1, 1923, was approximately 350,000,000 pounds, including about 75,000,000 pounds imported from the Orient, and for the following year consumption reached a total of 390,000,000 pounds, including imports of about 80,000,000 pounds. (Practically all imported peanuts are shelled, but for purposes of comparison these figures are on an unshelled basis.) With estimated production for the current season of about 238,000,000 pounds and with practically no carry over, it will require over 100,000,000 pounds of imported peanuts (unshelled basis) to take care of domestic requirements.

These figures show that the total domestic demand for Virginia type is far in excess of domestic production and would seem to indicate that the production in this country can be increased considerably at the expense of imports. But it must be remembered that recent imports from the Orient have been confined chiefly to large-size shelled Virginia type stock and this is the only class of peanuts for which there is a demand appreciably in excess of domestic production. An increase in production of the classes of peanuts now being grown would probably serve only to increase unduly the supply of the smaller-size shelled peanuts without supplying the large sizes which are now being imported. If foreign competition is to be met there must be greater attention to seed selection with a view to producing large-sized peanuts.

BEANS

A bean crop in 1925 in excess of domestic needs would tend to put the price of the entire crop on an export basis, thus losing to the grower the benefit of the tariff of $1.05 a bushel. If the usual acreage is planted in California in 1925, and if other States equal the 1924 acreage, a crop 2,000,000 bushels in excess of domestic needs may be produced. No increase in acreage seems desirable.

If an average yield had been secured, the acreage harvested in the commercial bean States in 1924 would have produced about 16,000,000 bushels, probably more than ample for our needs. Should California, where the acreage was cut in half last year owing to drought, plant her usual acreage this year and other States plant the same as last year the acreage would be increased about 10 per cent over 1924 and an average season would give a crop of over 17,000,000 bushels. The consumption in recent years appears to be something over 15,000,000 bushels compared with about 12,000,000 bushels before the war.

Imports of 2,000,000 bushels were required to supplement our crop of 13,000,000 bushels in 1922. With a production of 16,000,000 bushels in 1923 on an acreage smaller than in 1924 there were practically no net imports. The drought in 1924 cut the home crop to 13,000,000 bushels and imports are again heavy.

In sections where potatoes and beans compete, commercial growers who may be tempted to shift from potatoes to beans should remember that the present relative prices for these two crops are due to the lowest yield of beans since 1917 and the highest yield of potatoes of record.

The bean crop as a whole is made up of a number of very distinct classes and the price of a particular class may react more strongly to the supply of that class than to the supply of the crop as a whole. Adjustment of the acreage by varieties in adapted sections well within the limits of the 1924 total acreage would have a stabilizing effect on the bean industry as a whole.

Full data on production and price of beans by varieties are not available, but the information at hand indicates the following situation as to the different classes:

The production of the small white pea bean of Michigan and New York was about 10 per cent less in 1924 than in 1923, and only slightly above pre-war production. It is a staple variety, making up about 40 per cent of the total present bean crop, but its production has not increased in late years as rapidly as that of some other varieties which the market absorbs at higher prices. The facts of the general bean situation have particular application to growers of this variety and do not appear to warrant any increase in the acreage.

The greatly increased production of Great Northerns, chiefly in Idaho and Montana, seems to have been easily absorbed, and this class is finding a more ready market, at prices equal to or higher than those prevailing for pea beans. The production in 1924 reached about 1,500,000 bushels.

The production of red kidneys has increased about 30 per cent in two years. Prices in 1923 fell somewhat, and the present price increase no doubt reflects in part the general shortage, so that some caution would appear desirable in making further increases in the acreage of this type.

The unusually low yields per acre of pintos on the greatly increased acreage in Colorado and New Mexico prevented the supply from exceeding current requirements. The low California production of pinks and other classes of colored beans caused by drought in 1924 contributed to the present favorable price position of all colored beans, including pintos.

COMMERCIAL VEGETABLES

During 1925 there probably will be a sustained or slightly increased demand for such vegetables as lettuce, celery, spinach, and cucumbers but there is little prospect for any increase in the demand for cabbage and onions and for such staple canning crops as corn and tomatoes. There are indications that during recent years the production of vegetables has been increasing rather more rapidly than the demand and the tendency seems to be toward generally lower prices with increased competition between the various commercial producing sections. As vegetable crops are now being produced in many areas poorly adapted to their cultivation and poorly situated with respect to market, some readjustment of acreages to meet this situation is desirable.

Unusual weather conditions east of the Rocky Mountains in 1924 retarded shipments in the earlier sections. This interference with the normal marketing period brought some of these vegetables into keen competition with those from later districts and gave others exceptional markets. Growers should therefore avoid being influenced too much by profits or losses last season.

The acreage devoted to cabbage, onions, and other vegetables that have long been in general use has been adequate and any increase in plantings over those of last year should be made with caution.

The increased availability and use of other fresh vegetables throughout the year tends to restrict further increase in per capita consumption of these staple crops.

FRUIT

Present conditions indicate that increased plantings of citrus fruits and western grapes should be discouraged and that any plantings of apples, peaches, and pears, and other tree fruits should be confined to the best commercial sections and to the gradual replacement of old farm orchards in localities where a good local market seems assured.

Aside from the usual wide fluctuation in the annual production of all fruits, because of weather conditions, total production has taken a sharp upward trend the past few years, principally because of increases in the production of peaches in the Southern States, especially in Georgia and North Carolina. Increased production of pears has also contributed to this situation. Apple production has remained on a fairly constant level, although there has been some substitution of good commercial varieties for poorer ones in the older orchards and the proportion of the crop produced in the best commercial sections and in orchards large enough to justify the use of modern spraying equipment has increased.

Apples.—The immediate outlook for the portion of the 1924 apple crop remaining unsold is bright. The lighter crop produced in 1924 is reflected in the cold-storage holdings of apples on January 1, 1925, which were approximately 30 per cent below those on January 1, 1924. This lighter supply, coupled with a satisfactory economic situation at home and abroad, has created a good demand and caused a recent strengthening of the market, and it appears that present prices will be maintained or increased slightly during the remainder of the season.

As a long-time outlook a continuance of the practice of substituting the best commercial varieties for poorer varieties in the older orchards and the elimination of orchards planted on unfavorable sites seems advisable. In certain sections where growing conditions are especially favorable and where there is a suitable market outlet it is probable that small net increases in plantings may be justified, especially where direct marketing in towns of a few thousand population not now well supplied with high-grade fruit is possible.

Peaches.—The situation with regard to peaches is somewhat the same as for apples. In general such new plantings as are made should be confined to the renewals of older orchards and only standard varieties should be used. Replacement in the Southern States, at least in the southeastern group, should generally be discontinued for the next year or two, as it is doubtful whether a full crop produced from present plantings can be marketed at prices profitable to growers. Any replantings that may be made in that section should be confined to areas and land especially well-suited to peach production and early-maturing varieties should be avoided for the most part.

Growers in northern sections who contemplate new plantings of early maturing varieties should study carefully the possible competition of the more popular later varieties in southern districts. In many sections there is a conspicuous need of attention to standardization of pack and grade in the peach industry.

Grapes.—Grape production in California is increasing rapidly as the result of heavy plantings of raisin grapes and to a lesser extent of table and juice grapes, during the past few years. Production will continue upward for several years even without additional plantings, as many new plantings have not yet come into bearing. The yield of the 1924 crop in California was reduced by the drought and the full effect of average production from the increased plantings in that State has not yet been felt upon the market.

This increasingly heavy production in sight in California during the next few years gives no promise of anything except a continuation of the generally unsatisfactory prices which have prevailed there for the past few years. In view of this situation it is believed that no new plantings should be undertaken at present.

Prices in recent years generally have been more satisfactory to eastern grape producers than to those in California, but the effect of heavy supplies from California can not be ignored and it is probable that the general price level for grapes will be lower during the next few years. This fact should be considered by eastern growers before any new plantings are attempted, although it is believed that in particularly favored eastern sections some increase in acreage may profitably be undertaken.

Citrus fruits.—Unless per capita consumption of citrus fruits increases considerably and foreign markets are developed rapidly the citrus-fruit industry is confronted with an exceedingly difficult problem of readjustment. With a few exceptions such as summer oranges, and possibly some replacement plantings, no new acreage will be needed to supply the market for the next decade, except in the event of a severe freeze.

Production of all citrus fruit increased from 20,000,000 boxes in 1909 to around 40,000,000 in 1923. If all the young nonbearing groves in existence at present are given sufficient care and attention to bring them into bearing and if new and old trees continue to produce at the present rate there will be a production of at least 70,000,000 boxes by 1930.

Oranges show the greatest prospective increase. New plantings of oranges during the past few years in California have been sufficient only to maintain the present acreage of bearing trees, but more than 7,000,000 trees were planted in Florida in the five years, 1919–1924. There are large acreages of young grapefruit in both Florida and Texas. New plantings of grapefruit in Florida have been at the rate of from 250,000 to 500,000 trees per year since 1919 and a total of more than a million have been planted in Texas during this time.

In recent years there has been a downward trend in prices especially of grapefruit and of oranges that are marketed during the winter season. Auction prices in New York for Florida oranges of Golden grade averaged $6.07 per box during the season of 1919–20 and only $3.27 in 1923–24. Prices of Florida grapefruit averaged $3.72 per box in 1919–20 and $4.55 in 1920–21 but only $2.98 per box in 1923–24. The auction prices for a group of representative brands of California navel oranges averaged $5.70 in 1919–20 and only $3.67 in 1923–24. Prices for the 1924–25 season have not varied widely from the prices last year.

There is doubtless a possibility of increasing the number of car-lot markets but it must be remembered that through redistribution from central markets citrus fruit now reaches practically every market in the country and the problem, so far as domestic trade is concerned, is almost entirely one of stimulating the demand and increasing the consumption in the territory now being served. Lemons and oranges are sent to market every month in the year but the bulk of oranges must be marketed in the period from November to June and practically all of the grapefruit comes to market during this period. The problem thus becomes one of stimulating demand, particularly during the winter and spring months.

It is to be expected that the growth of the population of the country will result in a corresponding growth in the demand for citrus fruits, but at present our population seems to be increasing at the rate of only 1 to 2 per cent a year. Thus our population in 1930 will very probably not be more than 10 per cent greater than it is at present, while the prospects are that citrus production will be at a rate of more than 50 per cent greater than at present.

To some extent the consumption of citrus fruits can be increased through the use of by-products. At the present time a considerable amount of fruit is used for such purposes but the by-products industry can never be expected to take more than a relatively small amount of the fruit.

The United States may look for increased exports in her citrus fruits. In 1924 the total oranges exported amounted to over 2,500,000 boxes. This is only a small amount of the total production but the potential demand is of considerable importance.

Most of this fruit went to Canada. The exports of citrus fruits to European countries is at present difficult because of competition with producing areas in the Mediterranean district, Palestine, and South Africa. Transportation, especially from the Mediterranean countries, is at a cost much lower than from the United States to the various consuming centers in northern European markets.

The immediate foreign situation seems to favor an improvement in the market for lemons. Production of lemons in Italy, the chief competitor of the United States in domestic markets as well as in Canada, appears to be declining. There also seems to be some prospect for an improvement in European economic conditions which will increase the European demand for lemons and afford some relief to the United States by taking more Italian lemons off the domestic and Canadian markets. A relief from competition in these markets would turn over to American producers a market which now takes about a million and a half boxes.

The problem of the foreign market for grapefruit is primarily that of creating a demand. In increasing sales in Europe it is necessary both to develop the European taste for grapefruit and to find economical methods of marketing which make it possible to sell at relatively low prices.

TOBACCO

The price outlook for most types of tobacco is better now than a year ago. While stocks held by dealers and merchants on October 1, 1924, were 163,000,000 pounds larger than a year previous, the 1924 crop was 272,000,000 pounds less, a net decrease of 109,000,000 pounds, or 3 per cent, in the total supplies as of October 1, 1924. The current price per pound for most types is as good or better than one year ago, and there is no apparent indication of a slackening of domestic or foreign demand for tobacco.

Domestic manufacture of cigarettes in 1924 has been estimated at 71,000,000,-000, compared with 65,000,000,000 in 1923; manufacture of smoking, plug, and snuff in 1924 was much greater than the previous year. Exports in 1924 were 547,000,000 pounds, or 15 per cent greater than in the previous year.

Cigarette types.—The situation as to the different cigarette types differs radically. Burley, which is important in cigarette manufacture, is at present almost negligible in exports. The production of this type in 1923 was extremely heavy and decreased only moderately in 1924. The accumulated holdings of burley of 428,000,000 pounds on October 1, 1924, were 25 per cent larger than in 1923, so that its market situation is the least satisfactory of the cigarette types. The increasing consumption of cigarettes, and steps recently taken to stimulate foreign sales, may reduce stocks of this tobacco during 1925; but the general situation is not such as to warrant an increase in the acreage planted to burley in 1925.

The price per pound to the growers will probably not vary much from last year. The crop in the main producing sections is somewhat shorter than last year owing to drought, but the crop has more body.

Flue-cured tobacco is in an unusually strong position, due not only to the fact that it shares in the increasing manufacture of cigarettes and is one of the important export types, but also to the reduced acreage and low average yield in 1924. Total supplies on October 1, 1924, were 10 per cent less than a year previous. Exports during 1924 were 35 per cent greater than in 1923. Should exports in 1925 equal those of 1924, there will remain from the latest crop to supply the domestic needs less than 176,000,000 pounds, compared with 327,000,000 pounds of the 1923 crop.

The heaviest importers of this type are England, China, and Germany, in which countries there is now no indication of a slackening demand. It is significant also that in other countries, such as Canada, British India, Japan, and Australia, importations are increasing.

The price per pound to growers for the 1924 crop is several cents per pound higher than a year ago.

Maryland and eastern Ohio export.—Demand for Maryland and eastern Ohio export type of tobacco in the last few years has been strengthened because the domestic demand for use in cigarette blends now competes with the long-established export business for this tobacco.

Dark tobacco.—The statistical position of this group taken as a whole, is stronger than that of other groups. The total supplies at the close of 1924 show a reduction of 56,000,000 pounds, or 9 per cent from the high point of 1923, whereas the exports in 1924 showed an increase of about 10 per cent over 1923. Should exports in 1925 equal those of last year, there will remain from the 1924 crop for domestic consumption about 72,000,000 pounds compared with 149,000,000 pounds of the 1923 crop, and 155,000,000 pounds of the 1922 crop. The bulk of the exports are provided by the Clarksville and Hopkinsville, the Mayfield and Paducah and Virginia Dark. The production of the last-named type has declined moderately in the last year, that of the other two types has fallen off about 18 per cent. The remaining dark tobacco types have decreased in production about 31 per cent in 1924 compared with 1923. There is nothing to indicate that foreign demand will not continue good for dark types, although it is to be noted that production of dark tobacco in European countries is on an upward trend.

The general outlook for dark tobacco does not suggest material changes from last year's plantings, but it does offer hopes for improved prices for the 1924 crop, and a still further reduction in the holdings on October 1, 1925.

Cigar Types.—The outlook for cigar leaf suitable for wrappers, binders, and fillers of next year's crop is strengthened by decreased production and the unusually large percentage of the last crop that has been damaged and will be used for stemming. Of the crop produced, that in Wisconsin is the poorest in quality reported in many years. Considerable hail damage was done to the Connecticut Valley crop.

SUGAR

The 14 per cent increase in world sugar production for the season 1924–25 over the previous record production in 1923–24 caused a distinct decline in world prices. Since cane sugar production, which furnishes about 80 per cent of the sugar supply of the United States, does not respond quickly to price changes, the production of 1925–26 is also likely to be large. With a probability of a large carry over to cover the demands of the early part of the season of 1925–26, the chances of higher prices for sugar and sugar beets during the coming season seem remote.

World production of sugar, both beet and cane, for the season 1924–25 is now estimated at 25,134,000 short tons, as compared with the previous record production of 22,054,000 short tons in 1923–24. Cane sugar production is estimated at 16,455,000 short tons, an increase of 5.8 per cent over last year and beet sugar at 8,679,000 short tons, an increase of 33.5 per cent over last year. The largest increases are in the European beet sugar areas. All of the leading cane sugar surplus areas outside of the United States show material increases in production over last year.

Sugar production in continental United States amounted to about 1,200,000 short tons in 1924–25, as compared with 1,043,000 short tons in 1923–24; Hawaii will probably produce about the same as last year; Porto Rico shows an increase of about 75,000 short tons; and reports from the Philippines indicate a large increase in production, although definite figures are not available.

Cuban sugar production in 1924–25 is estimated at more than 5,200,000 short tons, which is an increase of 600,000 short tons over the crop of the previous year, and 1,000,000 short tons over the crop of 1922–23. As far as dutiable sugar is concerned the Cuban crop, enjoying tariff preference, dominates the sugar situation in the United States.

European countries outside of Russia and Poland have practically reached pre-war production, and with lower prices this year a further general increase in production next year would seem unlikely. Cane sugar producing countries, which increased acreage during the war period to supply the deficit caused by the loss of the beet-sugar areas of Europe, have not increased production as rapidly in the last few years, and present prices are not likely to stimulate further plantings. Immediate reduction in sugar-cane acreage, however, is unlikely because of the charcter of cane cultivation in tropical countries.

Until the present season, world consumption of sugar has kept pace with the rapid increase in world production, and at the beginning of the season 1924-25 stocks were low in Cuba, and in the leading European countries stocks on September 1, 1924, were only about 600,000 short tons as compared with 770,000 short tons on the same date both in 1922 and 1923. It is expected that, with lower prices prevailing, there will be a further increase in consumption but hardly sufficient to absorb the increase of 14 per cent in the supply. A part of this supply therefore will doubtless go to increase stocks and so enter into competition with the crop of 1925-26.

RICE

During recent years the United States has exported about 50 per cent of its rice crop, and the price of rice in this country has been determined chiefly by the production in the foreign countries with which our exported rice competes. The world's rice crop in 1924 was somewhat larger than the crop of 1923, but not up to the record crop of 1922. The acreage in the United States was slightly less in 1924 than in the preceding year, and considerably less than in 1922. The world acreage, however, has shown but a slight decrease below 1922, and has even increased slightly over 1923.

The tendency seems to be to decrease the rice acreage in this country and to increase it in foreign countries. The prevailing price of rice is about 25 per cent higher than the price a year ago, which may lead to a further increase in the acreage in foreign countries, and make inadvisable any considerable increase in the production of the United States.

ADDITIONAL COPIES
OF THIS PUBLICATION MAY BE PROCURED FROM
THE SUPERINTENDENT OF DOCUMENTS
GOVERNMENT PRINTING OFFICE
WASHINGTON, D. C.
AT
5 CENTS PER COPY

▽

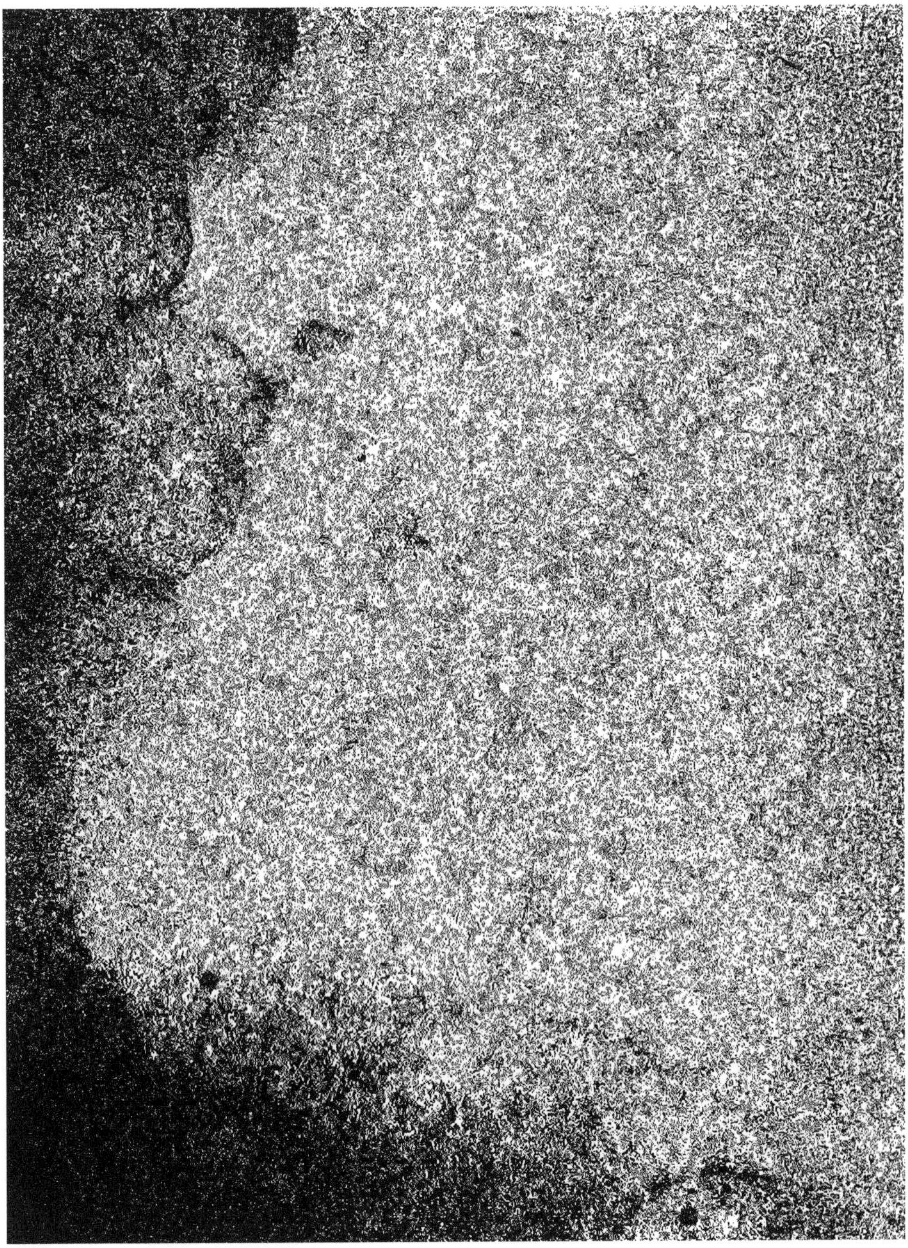

CPSIA information can be obtained
at www.ICGtesting.com
Printed in the USA
BVHW08s1102170918
527713BV00021B/570/P

9 780266 086031